GW00864463

Dream club

Dream club

Copyright © 2022 Jaiveer Asthana

ISBN: 9798431645532

Author: Jaiveer Asthana

Cover and design: Katrina Ravn

Illustrations: Jessica Ly, Juana Garcia Gonzalez
and Phoebe Oflynn

DEDICATION

I would like to tribute this book to my sister who listened to all the nonsensical dreams I told her while growing up and the one thing I will never forget is the dream that she told me she had! "Jaivu, I had this dream that you made me a good cup of coffee." Yep that's it. One day I'll finally be able to make her dream come true.

TABLE OF CONTENTS

INTRODUCTION

To be honest with you I really didn't want to write a kid's book, I wanted to write fantasy action, murder mysteries or even romantic comedies. However, something massive happened in all of our lives, the pandemic hit and everyone was put into a state of fear. No one alive had ever dealt with anything like this! I was working in a primary school when this happened and without even trying everyone in the world including my students became part of human history. There were fights over toilet paper in the supermarkets as people began to panic buy anything in sight, everything closed, even the schools. For a time, things were great. We all thanked the gods for the beautiful weather and our subscription to Netflix. Eventually people began to get bored, everyone was tired of talking about whether Carol Baskins actually did it or not. Ri-

"However, something massive happened in all of our lives, the pandemic hit and everyone was put into a state of fear. No one alive had ever dealt with anything like this!"

ots were the next thing as people began to come together to stand for equality, content exploded on social media as big media had to pause production. Humanity tried it's best to keep morale up but things were very difficult. We are social creatures, lockdown was not good for us. I missed my friends and I especially missed my work, I was the Learning support worker for year 5. I had known these kids from the time they were 6 years old (year 2). I made a promise to myself that when I returned, I would do my best to put them at ease. My plan was simple: I would listen to them, find out what was actually bothering them and then give them methods on how to deal with the issues themselves. What I didn't expect was how badly this time away in isolation had actually affected them. They were stressed, afraid, unhappy and it was coming out in their dreams. This book is a compilation of the dreams of three of my students which they shared with me during our SALT (speech and language therapy) and the explanation that google gave us of their meanings.

All the names will be changed to protect the identities of the pupils however they will definitely know who they are by the names I have picked for them!

Drawing: The children's artistic interpretations of Mr Jay

The dream club

— MEET THE GROUP —

MEET THE GROUP

The first child I want to introduce is called:

OAKLEY (OAK)

Favourite food: pizza or his nan's spinach and cheese thingy that she makes when he stays over.

Interests: video games (Minecraft, Road Blocks and WWE 2k14) Pokemon and recently Dragonball Super

Favourite character: Goku, Pikachu and the Undertaker (he copied that one from me)

Classroom antics: Once got so excited that he started to shiver! We were going to the aquarium so I get it.

Random tit bit: Has only watched Super and skipped the original and Z and and! He said the Dragonball Z intro was lame. We almost had a falling out over this. It's a classic how can you not like "Rock the dragon"?

The second child is:

MYER

Talent: Can play the violin terribly as she gave it up in year 3.

Classroom antics: Told me when I asked her why she was being so mean to the new teacher, she doesn't know I'm nice so I can talk and be naughty and stuff.

Aesthetic preference: Didn't like wearing her glasses as she thought it made her look like a nerd!

Random tit bit: Always picked a strange character when we played dungeons and dragons e.g. a chicken. She literally picked a chicken without any magical powers or anything her move was peck!

The third child is:

SONIA

Favourite movie: Lord of the rings

Aesthetic preference: Came to Book day dressed as Hiccup

Classroom antics: Is frequently told off by the class teacher for being right

Random tit bit: In her spare time, she likes to read novels with a nice cup of tea! I mean what sort of ten-year-old likes to settle down with a cup of tea and a novel written by an old man in the 60's!

Drawings: Dream club doodles

The tall intruder and a secret mint stash

CHAPTER ONE

Oak's dream one
SHOCK WAVE

"So in my dream I am in class and outside I see this big light and I try and tell you (Me) but you tell me it is nothing and to pay attention to the lesson. I don't know what you are teaching but then I can hear voices and shouting. The whole room starts to shake and I try to tell you again but now everyone in the class is looking out of the window. There is this big cloud thing going up into the sky and then we are all knocked back with the shock wave of the blast. I wake up and everyone is dead. I try to move but I can't because my arm is crushed under some rubble. I'm trapped and then the rest of the ceiling falls on me and I wake up!"

MEANING OF THE ARM BEING INJURED
To dream of an injured arm means that you can't adequately care for yourself or possibly suggests your feeling of helplessness in reaching out to others.

MEANING OF BEING CRUSHED
To dream that you are being crushed suggests that you are going through a great deal of anxiety over a choice you have to make in the near future.

MEANING OF EXPLOSION
To dream about explosions means burying feelings, especially deep anger.

Oak's dream two
TALL INTRUDER

"This dream really freaked me out. I called my mum when I woke up and I couldn't get back to sleep afterwards. There was a man in my room. He was really tall and kept moving around the room like he was looking for something but he never touched anything. He came over to my bed and stood over me, I couldn't see his face, I couldn't move. My whole body felt like it was frozen. I couldn't do anything. He just stood there watching me. I shut my eyes really tightly and when I opened them again he was gone." (I'm going to be honest this dream made me very uneasy laying in bed that night!)

"My whole body felt like it was frozen. I couldn't do anything. He just stood there watching me. I shut my eyes really tightly and when I opened them again he was gone."

MEANING OF PARALYSIS
To dream that you can't move is a manifestation of actual situations in which your emotions and opinions are kept to yourself. The dream might also be mirroring your real body state, known as REM paralysis.

MEANING OF THE INTRUDER
To dream of an intruder means you are feeling shame and remorse.

17

Illustration by:
Phoebe Oflynn

Oak's dream three
SHADOW

"Mr Jay can your shadow do anything different to what you do? I had this dream about my shadow but it was doing different stuff to what I was doing. Then my shadow started to talk to me and told me to do the stuff that he was doing. At first it was funny stuff like dancing and doing like the Naruto run and stuff but then he started doing really strange stuff. I started doing the stuff but it didn't feel fun anymore and when I tried to stop I couldn't. It was like the shadow was controlling me. The shadow kept going faster and faster, it was getting hard to breathe. Then I woke up."

MEANING OF SEEING YOUR SHADOW
To dream of seeing your own shadow represents a hidden part of your personality or character that you are unaware of. These attributes may not necessarily be derogatory, but perhaps you are reluctant to reveal them to others out of fear of rejection or embarrassment.

To see a shadowy figure in your dream indicates that there are traits you possess but don't fully realize or comprehend. It can also represent someone who is immature, naive, and impressionable.

"Then my shadow started to talk to me and told me to do the stuff that he was doing. At first it was funny stuff like dancing and doing like the Naruto run and stuff but then he started doing really strange stuff. "

Myer's dream one
SECRET MINT STASH

"I'm in my bed and my mum comes running into my room to wake me up and we rush out of the house which is on fire. I'm so scared as I watch the house burning down with all my stuff inside I don't notice that the whole street is on fire. I run away and climb on top of a mountain so that I can see how far the fire has spread. Everyone I know is on the mountain with me. That's when I remember that the town has a secret mint stash that we can use to put out the fire. The mint is stored underground to keep it safe for when we need it but everything is on fire now and it is slowly coming up the mountain..."

MEANING OF YOUR HOUSE ON FIRE
To dream that a house is on fire suggests personal changes. If you are repeatedly dreaming that your house is on fire, then you might not be ready for the alterations and are struggling to keep them from happening. This dream can also represent the love and compassion of the people in your life.

MEANING OF USING MINT
Dreaming of using a lot of mint can mean that you are lacking spice in your life. Sometimes our dreams can reveal what we are deeply wanting. The spice in your life may not have anything to do with cooking but rather what you do day to day. You may be working too hard and need to take some time to relax, play a game, or see a movie.

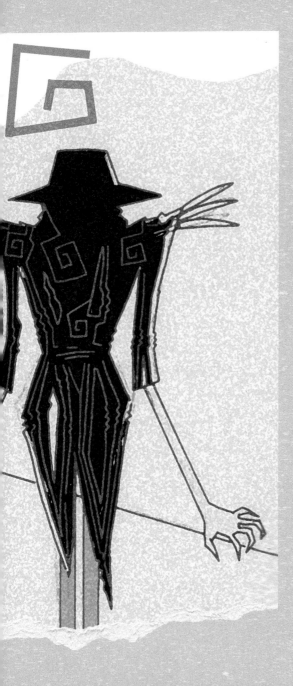

Illustration by:
Phoebe Oflynn

Myer's dream two
ELECTROCUTED

"This was one was a really short dream. So my mum told me that all the railroad tracks are electrocuted. In my dream I was standing really close to the tracks looking down at the rats that were crawling on the tracks. I kept edging closer to see if they were actually touching the wires when I slipped and got electrocuted. Then I woke up. If the tracks are electrocuted, how comes the rats can touch the tracks?"

"In my dream I was standing really close to the tracks looking down at the rats that were crawling on the tracks."

MEANING OF ELECTROCUTION
To dream about an electrocution suggests that a path you are on will go terribly wrong and could actually lead to your demise.

MEANING OF RATS
To dream of rats symbolizes the presence of extremely disagreeable or distasteful thoughts. Alternatively, it signifies feelings of uncertainty, guilt, envy, or other repressed emotions that are eating at you.'

MEANING OF TRIPPING
To dream that you slip on something implies that you are embarking on a journey or performing some action that you don't truly believe in.

Myer's dream three
HEAD SWAP

"I was a bird like a sparrow or something and there was a man that hated birds so he took me from my nest and cut off my head and cut off his own head. He then swapped our heads around. He started living with my family and no one noticed that he wasn't me. They saw this fully grown man with my head on him like he was actually me! Slowly he started to be mean to my family. I would fly past my house and see how horrible he was being to them. When he saw me he would come out and smack me with a broom."

MEANING OF BEING A BIRD
To dream of dead or dying birds is an indication that you may be facing misfortune or anguish. Minor troubles will consistently plague your thoughts.

Drawing: Myer's interpretation
of the bird head swap

MEANING OF SWITCHING BODIES

To dream that you switch bodies with someone implies that you secretly want what the other person has. Alternatively, dreaming of switching bodies with someone suggests that you are trying to understand the other person and see things from their perspective.

"I was a bird like a sparrow or something and there was a man that hated birds so he took me from my nest and cut off my head and cut off his own head."

MEANING OF BEING REJECTED BY YOUR FAMILY

Being rejected by family is a warning for your lack of power and freedom. You need to actively assert yourself and prove yourself time and time again. You are approaching a situation all wrong and need to look at it from a different perspective. This dream points at regret over your hasty decisions. You are unable to cope in some painful situation.

Sonia's dream one
HOSPITAL BED

"I had like a super weird dream last night. Woke up in hospital and I had all these wires going into my arms and legs (IV drips). Suddenly I was yanked out of bed by the wires attached to my legs and then I was being controlled by the wires like a puppet. That dream was really freaky!"

MEANING OF IV

Dreaming about an intravenous drip, or IV, is a symbol of being in desperate need of help, which you feel can only come from outside yourself. This need for help may be because you have let yourself become overexerted or exhausted in some way. You also have a desire to have someone else help you out of your predicament and come to your aid as a rescuer of sorts.

MEANING OF BEING
CONTROLLED LIKE A PUPPET

To dream of a puppet implies that you tolerate being controlled by some of the people in your life. You readily give in to the demands of others. You likewise feel you do not have a choice and standing up for yourself will be futile.

Illustration by:
Phoebe Oflynn

Sonia's dream two
LEFT OUT

"I was in my aunty's house with all my cousins and family around. It felt like it was Christmas or something like that. I was sitting in the living room and I could hear everyone in the other room laughing and having a great time. So I went in to see what was happening and everyone stopped laughing and just stared at me. I left the room feeling quite sad and went and sat on the sofa again trying not to cry. Everyone came into the living room and stood in front of me just looking at me not saying anything. I got up and went into the corridor, they followed me until I was at the front door. I opened the door and it was raining outside. They kept coming closer and I stepped back. I was outside, they shut the door on me and I began to cry."

MEANING OF BEING IGNORED BY YOUR FAMILY
If you had a dream that the members of your family are ignoring you, this means they will bring troubles to your real life. Most likely you will have to sort out their problems and settle their lives.

MEANING OF RAIN
If you encounter rain in your dream, then this suggests that it is time to communicate with others.

Drawing: Sonia's interpretation of being kicked out into the rain

Sonia's dream three
ROBOT PARENTS

"I came home from school and my mum was being really nice to me. She had made my favourite meal and kept a hot drink and a snack for me near my book which I was reading. I sat down and began reading when my dad came home. He was also being very nice to me. I was getting a bit weirded out by all of this. They were both smiling too much and doing too many things for me. My dad bought over a big fluffy pillow for me and adjusted the light for me. They just wouldn't stop smiling at me. This was making me really uncomfortable. Then I noticed that my parents were moving really strangely almost like robots. This feeling of unease was getting stronger and my parents movements were getting even more robotic. I stated to get really scared as they started making robot noises as they moved. What had these robots done to my parents? I was so freaked out when I woke up it felt so real!"

MEANING OF FAMILY
The general meaning of a dream of the family indicates that you are likely to encounter an argument with a family member. This dream also shows that you have a basic instinct to protect yourself.

MEANING OF IMPOSTERS
If you dream of an imposter, whatever the imposter is pretending to be is probably what you in real life are pretending to be. The dream imposter is showing you your self-image.

MEANING OF PARENTS
Parents symbolize safety and protection. If we dream about our parents often, that could be a sign of missing our childhood care-free days when we didn't have a single worry.

The big wave and mushroom eyebrows

— CHAPTER TWO —

Oak's dream four
FOOTSTEPS

"I have this dream a lot. Am I running but I have no clue what I'm running from all I can hear is the massive footsteps of like a monster or something. There are a lot of twigs and stuff in my way and I keep almost tripping over. I don't want to fall down because I know if I do I will be eaten or crushed. No matter how fast I run I can feel it catching up to me and soon I can feel it's warm breath on my back. I have never been caught in the dream and when I wake up I am always really sweaty."

MEANING OF RUNNING
If you are running away from something terrible such as a killer or monster this can imply worries and anxiety in life. The most obvious meaning of this dream is that you are trying to escape reality.

Oak's dream five
BIG WAVE

"I'm on a beach and there are people surfing on this massive wave. It looks really cool and I really want to try it. The wave just keeps getting bigger and bigger. At first it was exciting but as I saw it getting bigger I began to get worried as it was so close to us now. The people on the wave fell off and the people around me started to shout telling everyone to run away. I couldn't stop looking at the massive wave and I woke up just as it was about to hit me. You know how it feels when you wake up from a falling dream? That's how it felt when I woke up."

"You know how it feels when you wake up from a falling dream? That's how it felt when I woke up."

MEANING OF TSUNAMI
Dreaming of water that is out of control implies that there is a situation in life that is simply out of control.

Illustration by:
Jessica Ly

Oak's dream six
SPIDERMAN AND THE STORK

"This one is strange it's not one dream it kept changing. So first I am Spiderman and I swing from building to building. It's so much fun it feels like I'm flying like a bird and then I am a bird, like one of the ones that carries babies in its beak. I'm flying over the city, I can feel the wind in my hair but birds don't have hair and then I realise I'm not a bird and I begin to fall and I try to use my webs but I'm not Spiderman either. I'm just me and I'm falling and I'm falling very very fast I can see the ground coming towards me. Then it happens like always when I have a falling dream I wake up with a jolt."

"I swing from building to building. It's so much fun it feels like I'm flying like a bird and then I am a bird, like one of the ones that carries babies in its beak."

MEANING OF BEING SPIDERMAN
Dream about being Spiderman is a indication for instability and insecurity in your life. You are being pulled in opposite directions or you do not know which viewpoint is right. You need more order and organization in your life. Being Spiderman dream is a harbinger for issues you have with trust and feelings of vulnerability. You are trying to escape from the demands of real life.

MEANING OF BEING A STORK

It is a good sign to see a stork in a dream for people whose goal is building a career. This is a good symbol meaning successful promotion, as well as the emergence of opportunities to show your best qualities and abilities at work.

MEANING OF SHAPESHIFTING

To dream that you (or someone/something else) are undergoing a transformation, into another thing, person or creature, symbolizes a need for change from your usual routine. It also suggests your expanded awareness and a deep-level personality development.

MEANING OF FALLING

Whether it's real or perceived, falling in your dream usually represents a feeling of being overwhelmed. Maybe you're experiencing a loss of control in one or more areas of your life. It could be emotionally, or physically.

EXTRA ON FALLING!

Falling in a dream and hitting the ground is a concern a lot of people have. You won't die in real life if you hit the ground in your dream.

The science of falling dreams can be explained by a scientific phenomenon called a hypnic jerk. What on Earth is a hypnic jerk? A hypnic jerk quite literally "jerks" you out of sleep and into a wakeful state. It usually happens in the transition state, as you go from being awake and before you enter deep sleep. As you begin to drift off, your muscles relax. However, the brain misinterprets this feeling of relaxation and it may get confused, thinking that the body is falling. That's when a twitch or jerk is experienced in the muscles.

Myer's dream four
MASSIVE PARMESAN

"So you know that I love cheese right Mr Jay? I have lots of cheese themed dreams, I've had this one lots of times. I'm sitting on a table for dinner but it's not at home and there is a lot of cheese in front of me on a platter and I'm super excited to start eating them. Then suddenly I'm on a cloud and all the cheese is there but it's humongous. I choose the massive parmesan and try to bite it but it is too big for me to fit in my mouth so I start grating it and it starts to fall like snow all around me. I stick out my tongue and let the parmesan snowflakes land in my mouth. It tastes amazing so I start grating faster. Slowly the flakes start looking red and it tastes like blood. I look down and see that the cheese is gone and I have started grating my hand!"

"I stick out my tongue and let the parmesan snowflakes land in my mouth. It tastes amazing so I start grating faster. Slowly the flakes start looking red and it tastes like blood."

MEANING OF CHEESE
If you are enjoying the cheese in your dream, it is representative of this happiness and fulfilment. Your dream may even be suggesting that you try to return to the simpler things in life to get your life to its most enjoyable state.

MEANING OF SITTING ON CLOUDS

Dreaming about sitting on a cloud means that you are a complicated and unique person. You're full of duality. You have two sides. Dreaming about sitting on a cloud indicates that you have a complex identity that can often be difficult to stick to. You are all over the place and find it hard to make up your mind about things. You want everything and its opposite.

MEANING OF TASTING BLOOD

If you have dreamed of seeing your own blood, don't be afraid, because that is a good sign. In the following period everything you do will be successful. You will come stronger and wiser out of your difficulties. The following period is extremely good for career progress. Your peers love you, so you will become a leader easily.

To taste blood in a dream symbolizes an upcoming disappointment in close friends. You will not be able to understand how you could be so blind and didn't see what they truly think of you.

The big wave and mushroom eyebrows

Illustration by:
Jessica Ly

Myer's dream five
DUCK CHASE

"In this dream I have this dog and I take him for a walk. He likes to chase stuff and I can barely control him. He keeps chasing all the birds and he really likes the ducks. So I take him to the pond in the park and he jumps in and all the ducks come to him. I'm really happy seeing him having such a good time but then he starts swimming back towards me. He looks really scared and all the ducks surround him. They ate him."

MEANING OF HAVING A DOG

A dog in a dream is the symbol of protection, this dream is a simple warning. You should try to protect something in life. If the dog is friendly, then this suggests that someone or that someone is actually protecting you.

"So I take him to the pond in the park and he jumps in and all the ducks come to him."

MEANING OF LOSING YOUR DOG

Dogs in dreams symbolise someone who is protecting you. When you lose the dog in the dream it could mean that you fear losing that person in your waking life.

MEANING OF LOTS OF DUCKS

Ancient Persians believed that if you see a duck or many ducks in your dream, you may have some trouble in life.

Myer's dream six
MUSHROOM EYEBROWS

"This dream is a bit gross! Ok don't judge me! So I'm looking at myself in the mirror and I have this huge spot on my eye, you remember like the one that Rosie had for ages in year 3. I try to pop it but as I press it gets bigger and the harder I press it, it gets bigger. It's so big now I can't even open my eye anymore. I start to panic and I try to comb my eyebrows down to hide it. I look at the comb and it has these strange mushrooms stuck on it. I keep combing my eyebrows but each time I do it the mushrooms just keep growing back inside my eyebrows."

Drawing: Myer's interpretation
of the mushroom eyebrows

MEANING OF LOOKING AT
YOUR REFLECTION IN A MIRROR

Seeing yourself as older or younger, attractive or ghastly in a mirror during the dream are reflections of the inside and usually are tied to feelings of worry, guilt, or self-chastising behavior.

MEANING OF HAVE A STYE (EYE SPOT)

Stye in dream is an omen for your need for more leisure time or your desires to escape. You are prolonging a decision that needs to be made. Perhaps you have been sworn to secrecy. Your dream is a signal for unrealized and unfulfilled goals. You are ready to face your problems head on.

"I start to panic and I try to comb my eyebrows down to hide it. I look at the comb and it has these strange mushrooms stuck on it."

MEANING OF HAVING MUSHROOMS
GROWING ON YOUR SKIN

Dreaming about mushrooms on skin signifies power and the qualities or feelings that rule your life. You are seeking attention for the work you have done. You are feeling the burdens of growing up. The dream is a clue for life's anxieties.

Sonia's dream four
THE COPYCAT

"In my dream I'm just me and I'm doing normal stuff like I'm in school. So I'm in lesson and I have this like sunburn skin. You know like when you get sunburned and your skin starts to peel. So I'm picking at it and it just keeps coming off but in one continuous piece. Then everyone starts looking at me so I stop but it looks like I have an extra half of my body. The skin then starts to fill out and I have this extra half me and she starts to pick at the peeling skin and is then sat next to me. She keeps talking to me and Miss gets really annoyed and tells me off. Whenever I put my hand up to answer a question she does it too and Miss only picks her and she says exactly what I was going to say."

MEANING OF PEELING SKIN
To dream that your skin is covered with rashes or other skin deformity indicates that you refuse to accept the truth. To dream of peeling something symbolizes the shedding away of outdated customs, routines, and situations. It may also represent the fact that you are eliminating and dumping unwanted exterior pretenses.

MEANING OF A CLONE (DUPLICATE / CLONE)
To see twins fighting in your dream denotes conflict between your conscious and unconscious psyche. It suggests that there are issues and problems that you are not resolving or have opted to neglect in your waking life.

Illustration by:
Jessica Ly

Sonia's dream five
CREEPY CRAWLIES

"Mr Jay, have you seen Harry Potter and the Chamber of Secrets? You know the bit with the spiders, yeah? Well my dream was like when they get chased but the spiders are not that big but they are pretty big but like still normal. So in the dream I am in bed and I'm trying to get to sleep and I feel a spider crawl across my face. I sit up and turn on my light. The floor is covered in spiders all circling the bed. When I try and step off my bed the spiders all try to crawl up my leg! I really don't like spiders. I try and shake them off my leg but they cling on to my pyjamas. I run as quick as I can to my mum and dad's room and all the spiders chase after me. There are so many cobwebs blocking the corridor but I'm too scared to care and run through them. It's like the spiders are trying to catch me in their web like Frodo! I make it to my parent's room and shut the door and I finally feel safe."

"I really don't like spiders. I try and shake them off my leg but they cling on to my pyjamas. I run as quick as I can to my mum and dad's room and all the spiders chase after me."

MEANING OF SPIDERS

To dream of a spider denotes that you are being ignored and overlooked by others. Perhaps you feel that it is best to avoid someone or something that will only influence you negatively. The spider also represents female strengths and intensity.

MEANING OF COBWEBS

To dream of cobwebs implies that you are wasting your natural gifts. You haven't taken the time to develop these skills and qualities.

MEANING OF BEING CHASED

To dream that you are being chased indicates that you are steering clear of a circumstance that you feel cannot be overcome. This is generally a metaphor for a kind of insecurity. If you dream that you are being chased by an animal, your anger that you haven't displayed or acknowledged is placed within this animal. You could also be trying to escape some primitive urge or concern.

MEANING OF FINDING A SAFE PLACE

To dream of a safe haven place indicates that you have a positive outlook in life. No matter how bleak circumstances may currently be, you know deep inside that things will work itself out. Hang in there. Alternatively, the dream implies that you are trying to escape from reality. You do not want to think about your current issues.

Sonia's dream six
TRICK OR TREAT

"So in this dream it is Halloween but it's in like this alternate world where instead of going trick or treating everyone has to be asleep by eleven o'clock at night. I'm in my bed and I can't get to sleep and I start to panic because I don't know what happens if you are not asleep by eleven. I keep looking at the clock and it's only a few seconds to eleven! I shut my eyes and try my hardest to sleep but it just doesn't come. I'm too scared to move, I'm really uncomfortable in my bed, I'm too hot but I don't want to let any part of my body come out of the duvet. I don't want Halloween to know I am awake. I pull the blanket over my head and finally risk opening my eyes inside my duvet. (I feel something get placed onto my bed and I reach out and take it. It is a note and it says, Hello I am Death)."

This last bit I think Sonia added to give it a little bit of flair, I think but it's cool so I'm keeping it in!

MEANING OF FINDING IT
HARD TO SLEEP IN A DREAM
Dreaming about not being able to sleep suggests that you sometimes find it very difficult to talk freely simply by fear of hurting others. You are loving and selfless, you are ready to sacrifice yourself to make others happy.

MEANING OF FEAR OF THE UNKNOWN
In the majority of cases, dreams that make you feel scared, terrified, anxious or afraid in some way are described as nightmares, but some dreams can express your waking fears or anxieties in symbolic and thought provoking ways.

MEANING OF HIDING INSIDE YOUR DUVET

A blanket or duvet represents safety and comfort to hide behind or under it in a dream may mean that you fear the unknown. Like if your future is uncertain or you are worried about what a consequence of a certain action may be.

"I shut my eyes and try my hardest to sleep but it just doesn't come. I'm too scared to move, I'm really uncomfortable in my bed, I'm too hot but I don't want to let any part of my body come out of the duvet."

MEANING OF MEETING DEATH
IE THE GRIM REAPER

When you dream of the Grim Reaper or other fictional or fantastical creatures or characters, it means you are creative. Grim Reaper, the universal symbol of death, a dream of this character simply means a fear of death.

The slam dunk and magical horse riding

CHAPTER THREE

Oak's dream seven
MAKE A WISH

"I haven't had this dream before but I think it's kinda nice and I want to have it more! It was like one dream but like lots of little dreams in it. So basically, I go to a wishing well and I throw in a coin but I realised that now I don't have money for chicken nuggets so I try and get the coin back. I slip and accidentally fall into the well. It's like the sea or something and I swim around and more people throw in coins with their wishes. Whenever I touch any of the coins I get to see their wish coming true! One guy wished for a pet Bully XL like the one I got but couldn't keep because of my allergies. Then another one wanted a PS5 and another one wanted to go to Disneyland but the one that was in America. I liked this dream."

DREAMING OF SWIMMING
Dreaming of swimming in clear blue water where everything is visible means that you feel that there are good times ahead.

DREAMING OF A WISHING WELL
Dreams of a wishing well are a sign of good luck that you are in the process of making your hopes and dreams a reality!

DREAMING ABOUT THROWING
A COIN IN A WISHING WELL
Coin tossed into a river or a wishing well can be interpreted as making decisions and mistakes in life. It can also symbolize contemplation over a given crucial description.

Oak's dream eight
SLAM DUNK

"Mr Jay, do you know the anime Kuroko no basket? So in this dream I was playing basketball in the playground with the guys and then Mo passed me the ball and I could see that Ezra was open so I passed it to him. But then everything switched and I was in the anime and I had the ball and I could see that Tiga (one of the main characters of the anime) was open and I did that epic no look pass that Kurokochi does and Tiga dunks the ball in."

MEANING OF PLAYING BASKETBALL
To dream of a basketball game represents a struggle to prove that your ideas are better than other people's ideas. Struggling to prove you are right or more deserving of respect than someone else. Proving you are smarter. Using all your skills, ideas, insights, or resources to prove someone else wrong.

MEANING OF BEING IN A CARTOON/ANIME
If you see a certain cartoon or anime character in your dream it might mean that you are seeing them as someone from your waking life. The character may share the same characteristics or personality traits as someone in your life.

MEANING OF WINNING A GAME
Winning or scoring in a game could mean that you are feeling confident in the upcoming events in your life. If you are assisting in the victory e.g. passing the ball or blocking a intervening player you feel that you are a valuable person in your social circles.

Oak's dream nine
BOAT FIGHT SCENE

"So I'm like a really rich guy like a billionaire or something and I'm on like this really big boat you know like a yacht or something. There is lots of food and I'm driving the ship. It's a really nice day, it's super sunny and I can see dolphins in the sea jumping out of the water to keep up with the ship. Then suddenly this like assassin guy comes up behind me and tries to kill me. But I grab him and throw him off the side but he flips back into the ship. Then the robot that I made comes and helps me and we fight off the assassin. The robot does the choke-slam on him and I pin him. You know, like a tag team match in WWE." (I'm guessing the robot did the 3 count.)

MEANING OF BEING RICH
To dream of being rich means that you hope for success and wealth in life and want to work hard towards achieving this goal. It could also mean that you would like more financial gain in your waking life but are unable to do so currently. Dreaming of wealth and living a luxurious life may also mean you are an ambitious and driven person who aims to be free of financial burdens that may exist in your waking life.

MEANING OF BEING ON A SHIP/YACHT
Being in a yacht in your dream, or even owning a yacht suggests that you are an open person, you are sociable, and have many initiatives. Sailing in a yacht on calm waters is the omen of happiness, as well as good business. Owning a yacht means that you are confident in regard to your future and your talents.

MEANING OF BRIGHT SUNNY DAY
Sunny day mean pleasure and enjoyment in your life

MEANING OF SEEING DOLPHINS
Dolphins are a symbol for guides and protectors seeing them in your dreams may mean that you have someone you trust watching over you, making you feel safe in your chosen path in life.

"I can see dolphins in the sea jumping out of the water to keep up with the ship. Then suddenly this like assassin guy comes up behind me and tries to kill me."

MEANING OF FIGHTING FOR YOUR LIFE
Fighting a stranger in the dream is fighting yourself. This dream is about the fact that you need to keep on trying in life no matter how hard things get. If you win the fight it means that you don't want to give up and will come up with solutions to solve any problems we might be facing.

MEANING OF HAVING A ROBOT
Dreaming about being friends with a robot may mean that you feel alone or that you lack real friends and must rely on an artificial being to come to your aid. Having a robot that displays human characteristics could also mean you have someone in your life that will do anything that you require of them. If you are the creator of the robot it may mean that you like to have control over the people in your life.

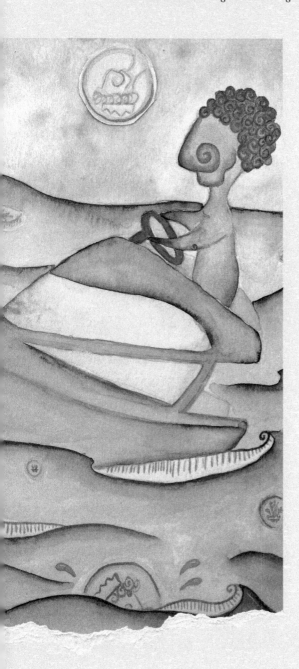

Illustration by:
Juana Garcia
Gonzalez

Myer's dream seven
SNOWBALL DOMINOES

"I know it's not even cold now but I had this dream last night about having a massive snowball fight! So it starts off when I'm walking home and there is snow everywhere and it's really deep like up to my knees. A snowball going wizzing past my head and I turn around to see who threw it but there is no one there. I see someone's hat poking out from behind a tree and as soon as I do hundreds of snowballs come flying towards me and I duck and roll and dodge all of them. I start throwing snowballs back at them and every time I throw I hit them right in the head, it's like I have ice powers! Soon I don't even have to bend down to pick up the snow. I can just fire snowballs straight out of my hands. I throw my last snowball and it hits this guy in the head and he falls into this other guy and he goes into someone else and it's like dominoes. Then I'm watching dominoes being knocked down like a big intricate one that someone took ages setting up."

"Soon I don't even have to bend down to pick up the snow. I can just fire snowballs straight out of my hands. I throw my last snowball and it hits this guy in the head and he falls into this other guy and he goes into someone else and it's like dominoes. "

MEANING OF SNOW
Dreaming of snow is associated with cleanness, clarity, and a possible fresh start ahead. A stage in your life is over and there is a new beginning coming. Since snow is water in solid form, it symbolizes something in life will take shape and be more concrete going forward.

MEANING OF HAVING A SNOWBALL FIGHT
Having a snowball fight in a dream means you have joy, passion and fun in your life which is expressed through the frivolous fun of a snowball fight. It may also mean you feel safe to tell people in your life your opinion without the fear of being judged or hurting their feelings.

MEANING OF HAVING SUPER POWERS
Having super powers in you dreams may mean that you are working to achieve your goals which you are finding difficult. It could also mean there is a hiding side to you that you don't want to reveal to the people in your life yet because you think they would be unable to accept you. Super powers are sometimes a symbol of changes happening within your bodies.

MEANING OF DOMINOES FALLING
Dreaming of falling dominoes may mean you have had a loss in your life, this loss is not limited to the loss of someone in your life but also of a failed project or cancelled trips/holidays.

Myer's dream eight
MASSIVE HAND

"So this is another one of my mad dreams, it's really hard to explain. So basically I go to the toilet in school and my hand gets trapped in the toilet door and it gets chopped off. Then this like new little baby hand starts to grow. Then it starts to grow and grow it's much bigger than my other hand. Then it's home time and I keep trying to hide my massive hand from my mum but she can see it from behind my back. Then we are in my house and my brother is laughing at my massive hand so I grab his whole body with it and now he is scared so I let him go and he runs away from me. Then I'm going into surgery and they chop off my hand and give me a new one. Then my hand starts to grow again!"

MEANING OF HAND BEING CUT OFF

Dreaming of having your hand cut off may mean that you are hiding some aspect of your personality or emotions from the people in your life. Dreaming of losing your dominant hand may mean that you are suppressing a desire or urge to do something important in your life.

MEANING OF REGROWING
A HAND (BABY HAND)

Regrowing of a limb which starts from the infant form to normality may mean that you feel that you feel the need to simplify things for people in your life. It could also indicate discarding your old way of thinking and accepting the new.

MEANING OF YOUR HANDS GROWING

Dreaming about your hands growing uncontrollably may mean that your creative mind and your logical mind are in conflict. This can be due to learning that the world is not just black and white but varying shades of grey.

"Then this like new little baby hand starts to grow. Then it starts to grow and grow it's much bigger than my other hand."

MEANING OF GRABBING YOUR BROTHER

Dreaming of restraining someone you know well e.g. your family member in your dream may mean that you want to understand you better or appreciate your point of view. You may want them to know something about you that they might not be ready to know yet.

MEANING OF GOING INTO SURGERY

Dreaming of having surgery may mean that you have a hard decision to make and are feeling differently than normal.

Myer's dream nine
SKY BEDS

"I finally had a good dream Mr Jay I'm actually really proud of myself! So I am jumping on my bed and I go flying up into the sky and land on the clouds. Where I can see an infinite amount of beds so I start bouncing from one bed to the next. They are all super bouncy and I can see a lot of stars. It's almost like I'm in space. Then I see these wings and I put them on and I start to fly up towards the sky but then my wings start to disintegrate, like Icarus and I fall onto a soft pillowy bed and get super bounced into space and I'm floating around looking at all the planets and stars!"

"Where I can see an infinite amount of beds so I start bouncing from one bed to the next. They are all super bouncy and I can see a lot of stars."

MEANING OF BOUNCING ON YOUR BED
Just jumping up and down on your bed may mean you feel stuck in your life going nowhere but it can also mean you are trying to rebel against the authority figures in your life.

MEANING OF FLYING WITH WINGS

Dreaming about having wings is an indication that you are a protective person that has high expectations of others. Wings also mean you are a very sensitive person that is very empathetic.

MEANING OF SEEING YOUR WING DAMAGED OR FALLING OFF

Dreaming of your wing being damaged or disappearing may mean the loss of innocence. It can also mean you are changing and shedding your past to become a new version of yourself.

MEANING OF GOING INTO SPACE

Dreaming about going into space shows that you are highly imaginative and adventurous. Space signifies the great unknown and if you dream of it often it shows a want for exploration and discovery in your waking life.

Seeing stars and planets means that you are comfortable with the feeling you are having and have accepted them. You are also striving for recognition for your achievement that you have been working hard on.

Illustration by:
Juana Garcia
Gonzalez

Sonia's dream seven
HOT CUP OF TEA

"I feel like a real grandma for this dream! I'm sitting on this super comfortable chair with my feet up and it's lovely and warm. There is a hot cup of tea with steam coming up off the mug and I have a digestive biscuit and no Mr Jay before you ask. It wasn't a chocolate digestive, just a regular, plain one. The radio is playing softly in the background. It's one of my favourite songs, Mad dogs and Englishmen. And I just drink my tea and eat my biscuit and listen to my favourite song, sitting on my big comfy chair."

MEANING OF SITTING IN
A COMFORTABLE CHAIR
Sitting in comfort in a dream signifies that you are completely at ease and are relaxed. There is nothing bothering you because you believe that life is good.

MEANING OF BEING WARM
Being warm in a dream shows a feeling of pleasure, comfort and an all round feeling of well-being in a person.

MEANING OF HEARING YOUR FAVOURITE SONG
Dreaming of hearing your favourite song in a dream could mean that your subconscious is trying to tell you something through the lyrics of the song.

Sonia's dream eight
MAGICAL HORSE RIDING

"So I'm riding this white horse in an open field, you know like in Lord of the Rings when Gandalf is riding ahead of the riders of Rohan holding his staff, chasing away the Nazgul. It was so cool I could feel everything, the wind in my hair, the horse's hooves thumping on the grass. I was going so fast! I don't even know where I was going, I was just riding!"

MEANING OF RIDING A HORSE
Riding a horse can mean satisfaction achieved through hard work. Riding a horse well can also mean you feel totally in control of where you are going in life and see only positive outcomes in your future.

"It was so cool I could feel everything, the wind in my hair, the horse's hooves thumping on the grass. I was going so fast! "

Illustration by:
Juana Garcia
Gonzalez

END NOTE

There are still so many dreams that I would have liked to put into this book. I would have loved to speak to more children to put them at ease to tell them that all their dreams are normal and nothing to fear. Through the dream club the kids in my group really did improve. They shared with absolute freedom with no judgement from me or the other kids. Their sleep improved as their dreams became more creative and less nightmarish. The best thing you can do for your child is listen to them, if they tell you some nightmare they have had tell them about one of yours. To let them know that they are not alone. I was plagued with strange and vivid dreams growing up, even now I have dreams that bother me. A simple google search can put my mind at ease but the world of dream interpretation can be a very daunting task for a child. I hope this book will show your child that our dreams have a lot to tell us about ourselves and we should not ignore them. They are our guides and they are powerful!

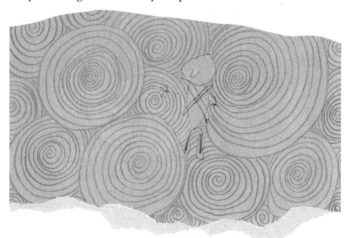

Drawing: Dream club doodles

REFERENCES

**Sites used for
dream explanations:**

Dreamforth.com

Auntyflo.com

Dreamsdirectory.com

Realdreaminterpretation.com

Dreamstop.com

Checkmydream.com

Dreamastromeanings.com

Luciddreamsociety.com

Dreamyobsession.com

Dreamsopedia.com

Dreammoods.com

Dreams.metroeve.com

Printed in Great Britain
by Amazon

78308946R00045